The Finish Line

Michael Shelton

Author's note

It was nothing personal. Ever since she turned me down, it's left me a mental scar that will probably never go away. It's there, I know it's there, and there's not a damn thing I can do about it. Whoever you find, they're lucky to have you. The only thing I ask is that you don't leave them scarred like you did to me.

I love you.

It was a warm California morning. The night before there had been an explosion which took down a building. While cleaning up the debris, a worker noticed a flash drive with the words "The Finish Line" scribbled on it. "Hey boss, you need to see this." Walking over, the boss looked at the dusty drive and plugged it into the computer.

In it was a story, this is what they saw...

It all started on a calm saturday morning. I was about 17 at the time, sitting on my porch, looking out into my neighborhood, where all sorts of things were happening. There were kids running up and down the street, dad's cutting the grass, and people yelling at their kids to come in for an early lunch. Then something caught my eye, there was a moving truck. No one has moved into the neighborhood since my little sister was born, that was eight years ago. Anyways, when I noticed the truck I had to go over there. So me being me, I couldn't just walk over there and see what was going on, I had to look like I fit in. So I got my bike and rode over there slowly. What I saw next took my breath away, there was the most beautiful girl I've ever seen. She was a brown hair angel and she looked like she came from a hot climate, because she was very tan. "Boom!" I forgot I was riding my bike and fell off right into her yard. I refused to look up, because I could feel someone staring at me.

"Excuse me, are you ok?"

"Um, yeah I'm fine, thanks for asking."

"Yeah of course, do you live around here?"

"Yeah, I live in that brick house over there."

I pointed to where my house was and saw my older brother and little sister play fighting.

"The house with the two little kids fighting?"

"Yea, that's my brother and sister."

"I've got an older sister.."

"Well, they can suck sometimes, but I can't imagine my life with them in it."

"I understand, Oh I'm sorry I never introduced myself, I'm Ana, what's your name?"

"My name is Ryan, where are you moving from?"

"California, my mom got a better job, so we had to move. I miss my friends, but glad to be in a new place, some things happened back at home....."

"Wha-"

I heard my mom call my name, saying that lunch was ready and to hurry up, because my brother has a baseball game.

"Sorry I have to go, but maybe tomorrow we can hang out, I could show you around the city?"

"Yeah, I would appreciate that."

With that I waved goodbye, got my bike and raced home.

The feeling I got while talking to her was something I've never felt before. Something about her. I don't know, really.

The next morning, I was anxious, how would it go? What could go wrong? Once I stopped freaking out, I came downstairs and found her standing outside waiting for me.

"Hey" she said, nervously.

"Oh, hey. How's it going?" I replied.

"Oh, it's going pretty well. I'm eager to get a tour of this place. It seems pretty intriguing." She said, starting to relax

"Yeah, it's certainly something. Let's go!"

Rolling out on our bikes, I felt near instant relief from any stress I had beforehand. I was with someone who took my breath away and from what I gather is a very friendly person.

"So where would you like to go first?" I asked.

"I'm not sure, being honest with you. Where do you go the most?"

"Well the museums are really cool and I have some discounts, wanna go there?"

"Yeah, that sounds like fun!"

I took her all around New York City and even went to grab a bite to eat. I went home that night happy knowing that I had just made a friend and I'm now way closer to becoming, hopefully more than a friend.

I saw her at school the next day and came up and asked her if I could see her schedule. "Yeah sure" she responded. Taking a look, I noticed that while we didn't have any classes together, we shared a lunch break so that's something.

After that I went to class and I couldn't get her out of my head, which combined with my already bad ADD, adds up to extreme daydreaming my ability to not pay attention. That leads up to some awkward moments when you get called on to answer a question you didn't even know was being asked. But oh well. Everything was starting to fall into place and I was all for it. At the end of the school day I went out to the bus loading area and went home.

The days rolled on with me planting little seeds subtle enough that it could go unnoticed, but enough that it was starting to shift her towards her being mine. It's a delicate process and all it takes is one time where she'll get suspicious about something and all progress will be lost. Once they've been planted, just let the time do it's work and take care of it each day and I'll be able to get her. Really it's easier said than done.

Also, something else I want to throw in there: standardized testing. Arguably the worst part of the year. You take all the shit you forgot at the beginning of the year, mix it up with some new shit that you don't get because you forgot the shit you were supposed to remember and you get a shit storm. However, navigate it with precision and you'll end up with great reward. All of this is starting to add up into an amount of stress and anxiety that some would say insanity patients had back in the 1950s. No matter how you spell it, it's bad. I think right now it's now or never. I'm going for now.

"Hey, we should study for exams tonight," I said towards the end of lunch.
"Oh yeah, we definitely should. As easy as the class is, we should go over the stuff we don't know." She said agreeing with me.
"Will you be able to stay after school?" I asked.
"No, sorry. I've got some stuff going on."

"That's fine. Can I get your number so we can study when we get some free time?"

"Yeah, sure." She said happily.

"Yes, these are the steps in the right direction." I thought to myself.

She was certainly something else looking back on it. There was just something about her that stood out from the rest. An X-factor if you will. When I knew her, it was right about the beginning of the freshmen year, when people were excited to see their friends when school had started. I had a leg up from all the other boys, she lives in my neighborhood and I had met and hung out with her although out the summer. So by the time I got to school, I knew that I was her friend and that was already something. By the time Thanksgiving was around the corner, she was calling me her best friend and we were hanging out almost every weekend. This on my part was an accomplishment, this beautiful girl is calling me her best friend, that's more than the other boys could say. The only problem was, I don't know what to do next........I've never done this sort of thing before. I finally realized that's what was stopping me from asking her out. As soon as I realized this my mind went blank, as if I don't have a plan to ask her out or at least figure out her feelings for me, what was the point. For the next month, I was trying to figure out if she even felt anything for me, I was starting to think she did... "Let's go see her." I said falling asleep that night, knowing that if I tried hard enough, I wouldn't be alone anymore.

That next felt different. I mean, it was a normal day, it was towards the tail end of the year so I wasn't doing anything important, but something wasn't right. I couldn't tell whether it was good or bad, but something was definitely coming. The best way I can describe it is being anxious for something that hasn't happened yet. It's kinda weird.

"Hey Ryan, I need to tell you something...... I really......."

That's the last thing I remember from my dream before my alarm went off. I got up, got dressed and went off to eat a quick breakfast. I met up with Ana, then we started walking to school.

"Ryan, I need to tell you something."

"Yeah, what's up?", I thought this was my moment, this was the moment we confessed our feelings to each other.

"I think there's something you should know," she said with a worried tone.

Me, instantly noticing this sudden change in mood responded with something like this: "Umm...ok, what's happening?"

"I've been doing some thinking..."

At this point I was thinking "GODDAMMIT SAY WHAT YOU NEED TO SAY!"

but because I was 99% away from success, I responded with a toned down version

of it "Yeah…"

"I like you, like a lot." she said with a relief of happiness.

I think at that moment, my brain exploded. Here we are, the girl of my dreams is

here telling me that she likes me. Not knowing what to do at the time, I fell silent.

I didn't know what to do. Do I tell her I like her? Do I just play along with it? I

went to class in awe. Did this really happen? Surely it's a prank or something. It's

happened before, it could happen again.

" Ana, I just want to make sure you aren't joking, because I don't want to say

anything that could hurt either of us."

"Ryan I'm not joking, I really like you, ever since you fell off your bike in my

front yard; there was something about you that makes me always want to be

around you and hear what you have to say."

At that moment, I was speechless, how could I tell the beautiful girl in front of me

that well, I like her too.

"And, I really like you to. From the moment I saw you, something told me you

were the one."

Well holy shit. What a day this has been. Now that we've confessed what we've really been thinking about each other, it really is now or never. There are plenty of opportunities coming up where I can take the leap so I am going to get planning on making that happen.

One day I came home and checked the mail, just like always when I sensed a presence behind me. Turning around to see who it was, it was Ana and she had a pamphlet in her hand. She held it out and said "My parents said that we're all going to get one. I can't wait!" Looking down at the small flyer, it said Do you want to boost your brain knowledge? Having difficulties learning? Then this is for you! It's the size of a grain of rice and yet it boosts brain power by nearly 300%! Never go to school again! Now only $399! Act now while it lasts! "I'll be gone about a week while it gets implanted. After that I'll be home." Clearly seeing the sadness in my eyes, she walked over, hugged me then kissed me on the cheek. "It'll be alright, it's only a week." I handed back the flyer, and asked "That's cool, but wouldn't it hurt?" "No, they numb you first at the site of injection." she said, trying to lighten the mood a little. "Oh nice." I responded. "I have some homework to get going on so I'll have to get going. That's really cool how they do that though." I said, trying to usher a goodbye. "Yeah. I'll see you later!" Smiling, I closed the door and walked to my room. I went to check the news when I saw something worrying. The headline said "Tensions are higher than ever between North Korea and the United States. Nuclear War is on the edge

now." Apparently something happened where someone was captured after

attempting to leave the North but failed and was executed. The Americans didn't

like that. So now my only friend is leaving (but at least it's only for a week.) and

now the world is on the brink of . I went to bed that night missing her already.

Today was the day when she went to get the implant done. On that

same day, two government agents rolled up to my doorstep and told me to come

with them. Pretty confused as it was, I got in the car with them and after about two

and a half hours, we arrived at this small, grey building. They took me inside and

into a room with a surgery table and put me on it and strapped me down. "Are you

sure this is the right one?" A surgeon asked. "Yes, he is likely going to have the

best chance at knowing how the chip works." "Alrighty then. Let's not waste

anymore time, we're already behind schedule." After that I don't know because

they put me to sleep. I woke up on my bed in my room. Strangely, no time had

passed. It was still 3:28 in the afternoon and I'd just come home. But there was

something odd. There was a metallic taste in my mouth and a really painful sting

coming from the back of my head. Feeling around to try and pinpoint the irritation,

I felt a small metal bump. I must have activated something by accident because a

display showed up and it had altitude, speed, it could see through things, it was

freaky.

One week later, I was on my way to school when I heard a siren. A WOOOOOOOOOOOOOOOO-WEEEEEEEEEEEE. Something like a tornado siren. Then, just overhead I saw a small white line that was creating a smoke cloud behind it. The chip clearly noticed what I was looking at and it brought it up. Is that a rocket? Why should we be concerned with.... Instantly realizing it was a missle, I got my bike and rod as fast as I could to Ana's house. I knocked on the door and she asked "Oh hey, how's it going? I was just finishing getting ready for the trip. My parents are out getting the paperwork sorted." Panicking, I said "Dude, you gotta come with me, there's no time to explain, come on." "What do you mean?" Clearly confused as to what the heck is going on. "I'll explain on the way." At that moment, the missile disappeared below the horizon just as the mushroom cloud rose up from a distance. "Nuclear warhead." I thought to myself. Not wasting anymore time, I grabbed Ana and ran. The blast will be here soon. I rode like a bat out of hell. Looking behind her and seeing the destruction approaching very quickly, Ana said "umm...what the fuck is that?" "It's started." I whispered to myself. After racing for miles, we came to a stop, safe from the radiation and the main blast. Stopping to catch my breath, we walked into an abandoned barn so we could catch up with each other. Turns out the implant wouldn't take very long and it took only one day.

The one thing I feared had become a reality. World War Three has started and my home in New York is pretty much no more. Ana and I were seeking refuge in a barn and we waited until it passed. Right as I was about to check the surroundings, I got a news notification saying "United States Falls as Washington D.C. is hit by Nuclear Missile."

Well fuck. Now the country has fallen into chaos. What a day.

I did a supplies run while Ana stayed back and kept a lookout. On my way back I saw a plane overhead that was probably Russian. So that was pretty scary. When I got back, we took inventory and we had enough water to last about 3 months and enough food for one year. But, as our little hideout was in the wide open, we had to move somewhere and quickly.

A few days later is when the problems started to occur. After Washington D.C. was taken down by another missile, the country fell into chaos. The chip that was implanted into Ana started to act up. Over the past few nights she has been talking in her sleep saying stuff like "The Master requests you." and stuff like that. During the day she gets a little pale and doesn't reach much. After scanning her for any diseases (which this chip is actually starting to be pretty cool now that I'm slowly learning how to use it), nothing showed up so I can only assume that the implant is causing this.

When a military parade came within an earshot of finding us, we decided we should get a move on to some place new. So we found a car, and drove all the way to the middle of nowhere. And I mean nowhere.

After about a week, we crossed the border into Kansas and found an abandoned bunker which we'll use to take refuge in for the time being. But Ana was not doing well. She was getting cramps, constant cold feeling, even if it was hot outside, vomiting, and a bunch of other side effects I would rather not dive into due to the fact that it is incredibly gruesome.

She couldn't take it anymore. On December 18, while sitting on the roof of our little hide-out, she said "I want you to end it. I can't take it anymore." Me realizing that it was the end of the line, I leaned over and cried. "I know, I know." she said sympathetically. "Is there another way?" I asked. "I don't know." she responded. "There has to be another way, there has to be." I said, trying to convince her otherwise. "Sometimes there is no other way." she said.

We went to bed that night knowing that we would be without each other for the rest of our lives and that was a tough pill to swallow. Mostly because I couldn't swallow it.

The following morning, as the sun was rising, we walked out to the middle of a nearby field. She looked at me with her big brown eyes as a tear strolled down her face and that was the signal that it was time. Trying to smile, she said "I love you, I always have, I always will." Raising up the rifle, I looked once last time at her flowing hair and perfect proportions. One shot was all it took. In an instant, her body fell motionless in the field. I knelt down next to her and cried. There wasn't anything I could do to reverse it.

Once I got a hold of myself, I took the body back to the bunker where I lit a fire and cremated the body, just like she would have wanted. I put the ashes in a small container and put it in an unmarked grave just outside the bunker. At that moment, I knew I had to avenge her death.

18 July 2064

"You can still save them…"

It came out of nowhere. Beep. He woke up tired and confused. Beep. There it goes again. He sits up and turns to the alarm clock and turns it off. Climbing out of bed to start another day.

It never changed the fact I took her life that day. It was something that will haunt me for the rest of my life. It was that traumatizing.

I got the chip implant a little over a week before the war started. I still have no clue as to why I was taken in, I'll just have to add that to my list of questions.

I haven't figured out all of my capabilities, maybe they should have provided an instruction manual for me to look over that as I got older I would become more advanced. But it is what it is.

He's lying to himself. He knows that it's all coming to an end at some point, the war will be lost if he does nothing. But he tells himself that it's going to continue and the war will be won, no matter what the price. They took the life of his loved one and for that, he's going to make them hurt.

19 July 2064

I've got no friends. In fact, I don't know anyone really. I used to live a fairly happy life. I had the girl of my dreams, school was great, just everything couldn't be better. But it's really not the same anymore. Which sucks...a lot.

I wouldn't say my life is difficult, because it really isn't. I live what I think an ordinary human would live. I wake up, check inventory, make plans for the day and just do whatever needs to be done.

That's a minor problem that I'll work out eventually. Probably when I decide to track down the company who started the parasite and destroy the servers. See the parasite isn't really a parasite in that it's a living organism, it's more of a computer virus that needs a host. Because it's a computer, it needs servers. Those servers are in a headquarters building somewhere that's not here.

Not that it matters, everyone is fighting with themselves, really. As for non-infected I don't know where they're at. I've heard about these "checkpoints" where there are rumors that there are those who haven't been infected yet, but I'm not entirely sure. The nearest one isn't too far from here, I get radio signals from there every once in a while.

I don't even know if anyone is looking for survivors anymore. Frankly I can't blame them. If nearly all of humanity is wiped out, then what's the point in using time and resources trying to look for the non-infected. The symptoms are so difficult to tell that you would have to know inside and out what the parasite does to the mind and body unless you have a struggling immune system then the side effects are quite noticeable, like Ana's.

Also something else I've been realizing is that there are constant changes in the sky. I know there's a term for it, but I don't know what that term is. I'll find it eventually. But there's a strong pull almost like a new gravity field that comes down in a tube looking thing and sucks up everything in its path. It's quite terrifying in fact. Which is why my little location is now built into the ground, about 5 feet under. Ok it isn't mine necessarily but you see the point. Now when they come I will hardly be affected.

It's an old base, built at a low point in the , there's enough supplies to last several hundred years. In all there are anywhere between 5000-15,000 bunkers and shelters to survive a nuclear fallout. There's filters, tons of water, medical supplies, the lot. Finding one is easy enough. Finding one in a decent condition, that was another story. He found one in about an average state with plenty of materials.

23 July 2064

A few years prior to the war, there was tension between the countries of the world. Everyone was standing on each other's throats and soon enough they couldn't take it anymore. The Middle East stopped supplying oil to the U.S. due to something (it was never clarified what truly happened) who was already having issues in Pacific with North Korea, who was backed by Russia and China. Once the oil crisis began, everyone scrambled to get the last of the oil. In his bunker, there were about 25 gallons of the stuff. Combine that with a faulty electrical system and disaster will ensue.

I don't know what it was, but the last thing I remember is a loud *BANG* and then my ears started ringing. The sensors clearly detected it before I did as before the brain part could catch up the computer side was already taking action on the nerves and before I knew it I was ducking for cover behind a shelf. I don't remember what happened after that because I think I passed out. But what I do remember is waking up to a lot of fire and smoke. The fire suppression system hadn't been checked in years so expectedly it didn't go off.

Long story short this is a complete loss and now I have to go and find a new place to crash.

As I packed up I picked up a picture of her and put it in a pouch for the trip. Once I had my rifle, some sort of experimental weapon called a "light knife," food, and water, I went to find a new place to stay. Before I left though, I kneeled at her grave and said "This is for you" and took two fingers and pressed against the burial site. He went on his way, determined to track down those who hurt him.

24 July 2064

I am considering seeing if any of these vehicles I've come across have any fuel in them. The one I used to come here is broken somewhere East and there's no point going back. It's quite tiring walking for such a long time. A good ballpark guess would say I've gone about 40 miles on the first day. Now night is starting to fall and it's starting to get a little creepy. I don't know if I'm hallucinating or what, but I'm seeing things that aren't there. My radio is starting to get low on batteries, so I'm only turning it on if I absolutely need to.

28 July 2064

Sorry it's been a few days since I last updated my status. But not a whole lot has happened. I came across someone who appeared to have just been killed, on the ground next to them was a little gray thing that looked like a grain of rice. Checking the database, come to find out that that is what the parasite looks like (which is what Ana had). This is good news because that means that unless he tried to dig it out himself, which I doubt, there are people around here. I've been in Nebraska for a few days now and it looks exactly like what used to be Kansas. There's nothing. Absolutely nothing. In other news I found an abandoned truck that had a full tank in it, along with a few guns. So sorry to the owner but if I don't find a new place to go then I might be done for.

Update: so I just arrived at an abandoned gas station that, knowingly, had no gas and there's something moving around that looks like a person. I'm going to go take a look and see if there's anything up.

As he approaches the weather torn building, he comes up to someone who appears to be normal, but unusually pale. He says "Who are you?" It responded by screaming and lunged at him. Reacting solely on instinct, he picked up his weapon and opened fire. Except the bullets did nothing but anger it more. "Umm, what the fuck?" He thought to himself. Pulling out a light knife, he cut through it like paper. It instantly dropped to the floor, a white liquid spilling out from inside. He searches the now dead infected one. Doesn't find anything that amazing, just a wallet with an I.D. Her name was Condolce Achbaker. However he noticed a pamphlet sticking out of her pants pocket. It was for the injection of the parasite. It showed a typical family having fun in a park of sorts, it said "Do you want to boost your brain knowledge? Having difficulties learning? Then this is for you! It's the size of a grain of rice and yet it boosts brain power by nearly 300%! Never go to school again! 23603 East NN Avenue, Los Angeles, California. Now only $599! Act now while it lasts!

Side effects include headaches, reduced senses, nausea, vomiting, and passing out. Keep out of reach of children. Not recommended for people younger than 21. Contact your local hospital if any of these symptoms occur and get worse.

Analyzing this new found data, he proceeds to the address.

29 July 2064

I might have myself a lead. When I was visiting that gas station, the attendant wasn't very nice, (I gave it a 1 out of 5 stars on Yelp due to poor service) but she had a little pamphlet that gave the address to the main headquarters for the company that makes this bug. I don't know how I'm going to get there, all the satellites are shot. I guess I could get a road map and study it and go for it. But I figured out how to transmit messages via Morse code (how 2000s is that?) and I sent out an SOS message to all of the channels that are still operating, hopefully someone received it. It just needs to be the right person. The last thing I need is to wake up one day with a bunch of infections coming at me. But I'm going to crash for tonight and I'll get going on the road tomorrow. My guess is that it'll take just over a week to get to what's left of California.

30 July 2064

Good news! I got a response from my SOS I sent out a few days ago. The response came from a few miles away at an abandoned missile silo. I've got their location and everything is in place for the likelihood that I would need to get out of there quickly. I don't know who they are or what they are really. But there's only one way to really find out.

Driving for a few hours and he comes upon the gate to the silo. He gets out and walks toward it where he spots a figure in the distance. Approaching the figure it seems apparent that they are on edge. Who could blame them? There's someone who just arrived at your secret facility you would probably be pretty nervous too.

"Are you the one who sent the message?" He asks in a concerned tone. "Yes." Ryan responds, closing in. "Are you being chased?" "I'm not entirely sure. I came across a few infected down the road but I think I lost them." "Good. Come on in, let's get you settled in."

Richard is his name come to find out. Nice guy, did a scan of him and as far as I can tell he's clean. Parasite free. Seems to have a little paranoia, but that's pretty normal. I mean if the end of humanity was happening, I would get a little paranoid too.

He invites him into his temporary setup. "How long have you been here?" Ryan asks. "Don't know. Since the war." Richard replies. "Damn, quite a while then, huh?" Ryan chuckles. "How do you get food? Water?" "Well I've got a farm down there a little ways and I collect water in buckets scattered all throughout, placed in 'strategic positions.' I then go and collect them when I do my daily patrol. You know, make sure nothin ain't be here that shouldn't." "You're not normal, are you?" Richard asks. "Not really. I mean, I have a 15 TB hard drive that gathers, sorts of data. Not just that but my senses, healing rate, metabolism, reaction times are all enhanced. For instance as I was approaching you I did a scan of you and your surrounding area to make sure it wasn't an ambush and thankfully it wasn't." "That's the thing is that they always know where someone is. They've got tons of satellites keeping an eye and ear out for those who might harm the servers." Richard respondes. "Is there somewhere more private we can talk, and maybe even get a bite to eat and a place to sleep?" Ryan asks. "Uh, yeah sure. Follow me."

1 August 2064

I've never seen a military base in person before. I've seen pictures and read about them but never have I seen a real one. That was up until this moment. See when I first met Richard we were at the main entry gate and because I would assume this is a secret facility. Nothing was seen for miles around. Also I looked over a roadmap of what used to be the United States and as far as I can work out there aren't any mountains in Nebraska. SO WHY THE HELL COULD I NOT SEE ANYTHING?

Update: Come to find out there was nothing within a 25 mile radius from the base for security reasons. Carry on.

Eventually the two arrived at the main part of the base and it was much larger than Ryan had ever thought. There were gas stations, restaurants, grocery stores, hotels, and most of all: houses. As far as the eye could see there were houses just everywhere. "Go ahead and pick one. Mine is just up the road to the right, third house down." Richard tells him, clearly noticing his surprise look. "We're they occupied before?" Ryan asks. "Nope. This place was built during the War. They had to make it appear as if there wasn't anything here. Like a little town or somethin. They did it in the World War Two back in the 1940s to cover up the factories that built machinery." "Nice. Well imma go find a place to stay and get settled." Ryan responded.

I never realized that there could be so many living developments in one place. They are just all over the place! Funny thing is that they don't look any different than the one beside it. They all have two stories, 4 windows on the front, a door with a slight left offset, flat roofs that are a light beige, with walls that are a desert sand looking color. I don't know what they called it because I wasn't able to get a proper reading for a color. On the inside there's a fairly long hallway leading to the living room. To the left of that is the kitchen and to the right are stairs. I counted three bedrooms and one larger bedroom with a bathroom. The walls are starting to show signs of decay from so many years of abuse with no maintenance as it sounds more hollow at random spots. Well I say random but they're occurring at 16 inch intervals. So I decided to take a closer look and come to find out that there are these brown boards that are called wood. Interesting material. Apparently it's all natural and comes from an organism called a tree. These "trees" are anywhere from 4-20 feet tall and have these green things called leaves. Then as the Earth goes around the Sun (I think) those leaves begin to fall. I know, it's quite creepy. I mean if I came across a bunch of body parts falling off an organism I would be pretty freaked out. But it's ok. That's supposed to happen. Another thing I noticed is that there's no furniture in this place. You'd think that if the government is going to spend a lot of money they don't have on something they don't really need, they could have at least put something in here. That's no biggie, I'll take a look around and see if I can find something.

Deep in the hills of California, he awakens on a lab table. "Systems Online" it says. People standing around it quietly ask "Do you know your mission?" It responds simply "Yes." "Good. The coordinates of his last known location are already put in. This is a simple exterminate and get out. MDS01302002 is too much of a threat to us. It's learning too quickly. It's only a matter of time before it starts comin for us." Says a scientist. "Take him out and come back." "Yes sir." The man who they call 'Master' walks in. "How can we help you, sir?" A nearby scientist asks. "It needs a name. Something evil, something that'll intimidate the people it fights." "Yes sir."

2 August 2064

I found some furniture and I can now live comfortably. I found what they called a couch, a table and a few other bits here and there to spice up my living quarters. Richard showed me around the place and now I have a place to work, as this place has a surveillance building. That should narrow the facilities where the HQ is and hopefully I'll be able to shut them down. It's actually pretty weird because you'd think that if they had been able to see our every move they would dispatch someone out here to come and stop whatever we were doing but I don't know really.

3 August 2064

I was able to hack the mainframe of the nearest facility and now I'm in the network. Come to find out there are 15 individual places with one main server controlling all the others. I reckon that if I can hit the main one, the others will crash before the emergency power kicks in. I have the address to the headquarters so I'll have a chat with some of the folks there.

"What did you come up with?" "We couldn't decide sir. So far it's a debate between Victor and Prileir." The scientist responds. "Well I like the sound of Victor." "Yes sir."

"Is it ready for launch?" Asks the Master. "Almost. We just need to upload it's data to the cloud as a backup in case something happens." The scientist says back. "Well get to it."

4 August 2064

So I sent out another distress signal to all the surrounding areas with the non-infected saying we have housing, food, water, etc. Hopefully they come. In other news it rained here for the first time in weeks. Turns out those weird gravity tubes I was talking about in Kansas are called tornados. Quite freaky stuff really.

5 August 2064

The plan was flawless. Take a corrupted non-infected and send them to the silo site to distract Ryan, allowing time for the death squadron to arrive. "Are you ok, sir?" Ryan asks. "YOU-YOU WERE TRYING TO KILL ME!" He replies. "Whoa whoa whoa, who's trying to kill you?" "THEM!" ""Hey man, just calm down. There's something in you that I might have to remove." "YEAH NO SHI-."

At that very moment a bullet goes right through his skull and falls flat, motionless. The robot reacted so fast that the brain didn't catch up for a few seconds. Now there were gunshots going off like fireworks. POP POP PAPAPAPAPA. On the hillside were at least 30 armed super soldiers. "Shit." Running back to the house, Ryan grabs his rifle, light knife, and two pistols and prepares for what's to come. "Everything calibrated?" The system responded instantly "Yes sir." "Good. Let's go. Wait, you can talk? That's pretty nifty if I do say so myself." Scanning the area he sees 15 people opening fire with 6 more scattered all around him, presumably to bring the killing shot. The remaining 9 were interrogating Richard. "Do we have a plan?" "There is a 15% chance of you surviving this. As of right now there are 1,500,258 different methods of taking them all out." "Well, pick one that won't get me killed." "Yes sir." On his HUD, there showed a trajectory path. Following it he heard footsteps quickly shifting. "There are two downstairs. Hit the one on the right with a blow to the arm and shoot the other one in the leg." "Let's go." Sneaking down the rest of the stairs, he leaps on to the one on the right, stabbing him in the arm. Screaming in agony he starts to work on the other one, shooting him in the leg. "Well what now? I can't hold them like this forever." "Both of them have the parasite. A blow to the right of the head will work. It'll overload the parasite due to the amount of trauma inflicted on it." "Well that would have been nice earlier. Looking around the perimeter of the house five more show up and a path of taking them out. Slowly exiting the building, he trips the first one and steps on his neck and hits him in the head, disabling the parasite. The second guy opens fire, alarming the remaining people. Now surrounded, he's got no other choice but to surrender. Or so they thought. The robot side is constantly making plans to any given situation and this was no different. At this point the human part didn't know what to do so he let the computer do the work. "Wtf happened. The last thing I remember is jumping on someone and then it blacked out." "Sorry sir, but your brain temporarily let the other side take over, as the human side noticed there was no noticeable way out. I recommend that you should relocate, this area is now compromised." "Alright. Will do."

6 August 2064

So I had to pack up and leave the base, Richard was killed when he refused to give up my hiding spot which sucks. But I snuck out using one of the numerous exits and now I'm headed towards what used to be California in order to see if that brochure was the right place. Also I just received a SOS signal from somewhere. I can't make out what it is. Another thing is that I found out that while I am still in control, the robot side is now self aware. Not to worry though, if it senses a corruption coming, it'll automatically shut itself down to protect me and itself from itself. Anyways I suppose I should get back on the road, I'll update this as I go along.

"WHAT THE HELL DO YOU MEAN IT GOT AWAY?!?! YOU

WERE SUPPOSED TO KILL HIM!" "I'm sorry sir but the robot part has become

self aware and it out-matched our best." "IT'S 20 YEAR OLD SOFTWARE!

DON'T GIVE ME THAT BULLSHIT THAT IT OUTMATCHED YOU!

CLEARLY YOU AREN'T ENOUGH TO COMMAND A DEATH SQUAD NOW

ARE YOU?" "Sir I promise I will get him. Just give me one more chance." "ONE

MORE CHANCE. THAT'S IT. IF YOU FAIL YOU WILL BECOME THE NEXT

TARGET FOR THE DEATH SQUAD." "Understood."

13 August 2064

I just crossed the border into California! Amazing what the effects of

nuclear war is on a place. I mean I've seen pictures of what California used to look

like, now it's nothing more than a radioactive wasteland. The ideal place for hiding

a place that builds parasites designed to corrupt humanity. But I'm going to stop

for the night and get some rest. I'll see what it looks like under sunlight. If this

place even gets any anymore

At that very moment a single gunshot is fired. Swerving to avoid it, he

crashes into a ditch and flips. Within seconds he is getting rained down upon by

bullets from all sides. "How many are there?" "12, sir." "How many bullets do I have?" Realizing this was a pointless question he checks his magazine. "Well I've got a full one. His many rounds do they have left?" "Judging by the guns they are using, not many." "Ok, I need a plan of attack here, come on." "Yes sir, wait until the cease fire and as the vehicle approaches there will be one with an exposed cut. Hit him there and use it as a body shield." "Oof. Alright then." A few moments later, with the truck filled with more holes and dents than the moon, they approach it. Just as the robot mentioned, there was one who had a cut on his leg. Waiting for the opportune moment, he jumps out of the cab and hits him in the leg. Screaming in agony, Ryan puts him in a choke-hold, with the surrounding assassins closing around in a circle. "What are you doing here?" They ask. "I was just passing through." Ryan responds. "Yeah, a huh. What's the map with the coordinates for?" "I heard about something there. Like an outpost or something. But really it's nothing. That was from a while ago." "Ok well you're going to have to come with us because you have entered a restricted zone" The leader tells him. "Well how about this then" Trying to talk his way out of it, "I just go the opposite direction back to where I came from? Never to be seen here again." "Nope. We need to know if you've seen anything you're not supposed to." Realizing he wasn't going to get out of this, he surrendered. Loading him into the back of the van, they set off to an undisclosed area. "Sir there's something going on. A strong magnetic field. My services might be of no use to you for the current time." Suddenly the van comes to a stop and when the rear doors open and he sees they're in an old hanger.

"Welcome to your hell, MDS01302002."

14 August 2064

Well I've been captured. Probably because of the stuff I was coming up with. But at least the holding cell is nice. It has white walls and floor, with the entire ceiling full of lights. There's a bed with some sort of cloth covering it, an automatic-emptying waste bin, and the door has a tiny little window in it, in case passerby's' want to take a look. But judging from what the authority figure said before I was put in here, imma be tortured. So if I want to avoid that, I need to find a way out of this hole. That's the issue I'm having is that the coordinates for the master switch for the servers matches the place I'm at right now which can only mean one thing: instead of me breaking in, they took me here instead. I need to get to formulating a plan so I'll update this when I have one set.

"Well I can't say I'm disappointed, but it took a lot longer than I would have hoped for." "Sir he's here. That's what you asked for." "Yes indeed, bring him in, I would like to ask him a few questions."

14 August 2064 (continued)

Ok so I have a plan for escape. The automatic-emptying waste can is connected to a number of pipes. After stomping around I've determined where there's empty space and where there's pipe. I still have my light knife, and I've marked where I need to cut. I hear footsteps so I'm going to set to work.

Working faster than he ever had, he cut a whole in the floor and jumped down. Landing into some sort of room with cameras, buttons, screens, and switches, he was able to locate an exit, but there were about 15 guards between him and freedom. That was the biggest of his problems. They had found out what he did so now the whole complex is under a code red. They knew where he was, they just had to look down. But how to access it was a different story. The guards were too big to fit and he couldn't fit down it like Ryan did. Their lives were on the clock now. Meanwhile, Ryan had discovered numerous holding cells with non-infected housing them. "You there." A battered and bruised head rises up slowly. "Yeah you, do you know where the exit is?" After what appeared to be a sudden energy shock, she instantly rose up and said "if you get me out of here I can help you escape. I know the ins and outs of this hellhole." After releasing her, they go and unlock all the other cells on that floor. "Ok, the exit is just past here. There's a door to the right, after that there's a long hallway followed by a series of tunnels. The one on the right leads to the outside." "Ok, thank you." Running down the hallway, through the door and the tunnels, he arrives to meet 5 armed guards. All aiming at him. "Fellas." Before he could even process the moment, he was already in action. A kick there, a punch right here, it was all over as soon as it began. Taking a van similar to the one that brought him, he drove straight through the gate and out into the wastelands.

15 August 2064

I escaped! It was a fairly simple process, seeing as they didn't do a very good job searching me I cut my way out. I lost some stuff but I'm pretty alright. I'm going to rest and prepare to go back. Why? Well those servers I keep talking about are there. And I'm not. So in order to shut them down, and essentially save America. Or the world. I don't know how far the parasite has spread.

"How in the HELL did he escape?" "Well, umm, he cut a hole through the floor and jumped down into the security room during a change in shifts." "You realize what this means?" "No, sir." "GUARDS!" Instantly, two guards showed up, ready for whatever task the master might throw at them. "Aim." "Wait Sir!" "Ready!" "But Sir please!" "FIRE!" Just like that the master's creation to exterminate Ryan was gone. "Call up the best scientists. Prepare for a public execution." "Very well sir." About 15 minutes later everyone was lined up on a large stage in the courtyard outside the building. "About 20 years ago you delivered the very first cyborg. Designed to exterminate the last of the non-infected, it defected. Killing our one. I give you the task of building another that can kill what you made. It defected, becoming too weak for our uses. You have failed me twice. Do you realize what this means for our future?" Nobody answered out of pure fear. "WE COULD BE DONE FOR. So to protect the company you are going to be terminated." "Picking up their shock axes, the exterminators lifted, ready to strike. "Do it now." Without hesitation, 15 strikes came down on the helpless scientists. Cutting through them like a hot knife through butter, 15 heads rolled onto the ground. "Now. Would anyone else like to confess to anything right now?" Nobody responded with the looks of terror in their eyes. "Good. Now if you'll excuse me I have a machine to track down."

16 August 2064

So in order to complete the mission, I'll have to act like them. So I need to make an entry card, get a guard identification number and such. The typical stuff. I'm going to get cracking. I'll update this once I finish.

Now security is on high alert. There's 24/7 guard patrol with a refresh rate of about 15 seconds. But he has a plan. It's essentially a suicide mission providing everything goes to plan. "It's for her." He thought to himself. As he approached the gate, he gave the guard his badge and let him in. In the back of his van is a bomb, one size down from nuclear. As he pulled up to the garage, he turned himself in.

16 August 2064 (update)

Whoa whoa whoa. Hold up. Chances are that you just read that I had a near-nuke in the back of the van I was driving. Ok I did but I need to explain how I got it.

So as I was fleeing the facility, I came across an old warehouse from World War Three. In said warehouse were a lot of munitions, tools, you name it. Well there was a bomb that appeared bigger than the rest. It even came with it's own instruction manual on how not to mess everything up. Following the instructions, I loaded it into the van, now there's a fully armed, near nuclear burrito in the back of this van. Then I also set the warehouse to explode. That's why there were so few guards and personnel. They were busy investigating the accident while they had to sub in new guys for the time being. After that I turned myself in, hoping to talk to the main guy, who they call the "Master." Maybe he's really good at life or something, I don't really know. Anyways, back to the narrator bit.

"The one I've heard so much about, MDS01302002." The Master said. "You know, it'd be much easier if you just call me Ryan, but I guess MDS01302002 works too." "Tell me Ryan, what did you come here to do?" "There's a long story to that, but for times sake I'll shorten it to 'I've come to avenge a fallen loved one." "I see. Riddle me this then. Your software is something like 12 years old, right?" "Right.." Ryan replied. "Then how did you manage to outperform all of our guards, and our best creation yet?" "Pretty simple, I learned how to code a short while after this whole shamble started, so ever since then I've been updating my own software as I grow up. It appears that I have outpaced you guys in the tech department" Ryan chuckles. "Yes, but I don't think you realize how much damage you've caused in your little plan of yours." The Master said in a cold tone. "We were approaching the opportunity to rule the world, and then you come along and mess it all up." "Well that was the goal. I seem to have succeeded. Isn't that what we all strive for?" "What are we going to do with him, sir?" A guard asks impatiently. "I won't be here long. I hope you guys know that." Ryan said, clearly showing his self-confidence in his plan. "Why is that?" The Master asks. "Because I've outsmarted you again. Right now, in the hangar just below us, there is a MOAB V2, or in other terms, the most powerful bomb to be built and not be nuclear. Found it in a warehouse from the . And right now, it's set to blow. And when it does it will take out the servers along with it, therefore destroying the parasite that plagues the Earth right now." The moment he finished the sentence, a timer went off. 'Beep beep beep beep beep." He takes out the guards and runs to the door. At this point, The Master shouts "You think this is the end? Oooooooooooooh no boy, this is just the beginning!" Running to a nearby aircraft, he hops in and starts it up. "Could you give me a hand here?" asking the computer. "The switch to the right is engines on, the lever in the middle is throttle control, the middle stick is to turn, or take-off and land." "Fair enough." Right as he goes to begin taking off, the bomb goes off, leveling the building. With debris flying everywhere, he's pulling away from the landing pad. But then The Master comes running from the dust and opens fire. PAPAPAPAPA PAPAPAPAPAPAPAPA! One of the bullets hits the engines, disabling it. With 50% of the power gone, he had no choice but to crash land. Despite the odds of him making it out alive would be 1 in 240, he took that risk anyways. Jumping out, he tackles The Master. They exchange blows until The Master pulls out a knife. "Well ain't that somethin. Cheater." he thought to himself. Knowing he was on his own for this fight, he did his best predicting The Master's moves, but the computer-operated machine he was fighting was just better. It was able to see moves before they even happened and with Ryan's energy quickly starting to run out, he got weak. Noticing this sudden change in effort, The Master knocked Ryan down with a powerful punch to the chest. Picking up the injured body off of the ground, he stuck the knife into Ryan's abdomen. Screaming in agony, The Master dropped the now powerless human. "I see great potential in you! Join us, you'll have so much more!" The Master exclaimed. "Thanks, but your advertising abilities aren't very good." Ryan replied. "You may destroy the "Master servers," but that's where you went wrong. I am the server. The parasite didn't defect, it was programmed right from the start. You were supposed to end them!" The Master shouted. "And yet here we are. Out here, claiming you're fighting for Ana but you're just fighting for yourself. You never deserved her." That blew the top for Ryan. Gaining back all the strength he ever had, he got up, pulled the knife out of his lower chest and shoved the blade right through The Master's circuits. Right after, a piece of debris from the facility came down on the now ruined cyborg, crushing him. "YOU--GO ROT IN HELL!" As he walked away from the collapsing building, he took a look at his wounds. The computer scanned it and determined that he wasn't going to be around for much longer.

16 August 2064

I can safely say that as I go down, I have successfully avenged Ana.

He found an overhand that faced the Sun. Lying down as a tear rolled down his face, he knew he had avenged Ana. As he started to black out, he whispered: Let's go see her, one last time."

www.ingramcontent.com/pod-product-compliance
Lightning Source LLC
Chambersburg PA
CBHW071118220526
45467CB00004B/1947